KNACK FOR LIFE: BLUEPRINT FOR SUCCESSFUL HABIT FORMATION. A PROVEN WAY TO GIVE UP BAD HABITS AND PRACTICE GOOD ONES

Take control of your life and Improving your life with simple steps to build good habits breaking bad ones. Become a free person and a powerful person by choosing your own feelings, words, and actions.

LANE BLYTH

Contents

Disclaimer

This book has been written for information purposes only. Every effort has been made to make this as complete and accurate as possible but still, this book should be used as a guide - not as the ultimate source.

The author and publisher shall have neither liability nor responsibility to any person or entity with respect to any loss or damage caused or alleged to be caused directly or indirectly by this book.

Introduction

The majority of what we do, we do out of habit. From the minute we get up in the morning, to the actions we take throughout the day - our regular breakfast, how we travel to work, - the daily habits we establish actually control about 95% our actions. These are all unconscious ideas that identify how we feel, what we believe, and how we act in almost every situation in our lives.

As our daily habits determine all the little things we do that comprise of our daily lives, they likewise are also connected to the larger things in our lives, such as the type of individual we marry, how much income we make, our physical health and body condition, and every other part of our lives.

Our habits and routines identify our character, the kind of individual the remainder of the world see us as, and, eventually, our fate. So, if we welcome bad routines, - those routines that have an unfavourable effect on who we are - then those exact same routines will prevent us from accomplishing true success in our lives, holding us back from reaching our maximum potential.

It's only by breaking bad habits and replacing them with good habits that we can eventually be successful in life, and be the individuals we were born to be.

The function of this study is to reveal to you how to break bad routines - any sort of bad routine, from those that are harming to your health, like smoking cigarettes or not using a seat belt, to those that have impact on your self-confidence, such as negative attitude, or overindulging, - and change them with favourable behaviours that can come into your life and cause you to see the outcomes you really desire.

You would have to be insane to believe that anything will ever change for the good, when you keep duplicating the very same bad practices. "Knack For Life" will reveal to you how to end the insanity, and begin living your life to its maximum, by deserting bad practices and exchanging them with favourable ones.

Wishing to Break the Routine

I wish to start with a story. Peter is in the region of 70 years old. For the last 4 months, he has been residing on a walkway the streets. I do not know the length of time Peter has actually been homeless. He is not able to look after himself, not able to deal with the business of life. One day I attempted to take him to a shelter for the homeless. All he needed to do was get in the pickup.

That morning he needed to decide: Get in or remain on the street. The best choice might have begun the cycle to healing, however, it was more than Peter could do that morning. He chose to remain on the streets, waiting on his fictional flight to El Paso.

I have seen how bad routines keep individuals from living better and much healthier lives. Many individuals would like to know why they are dissatisfied with live. And they would like to know what they can do about it.

We are continuously bombarded by quick fix programs that guarantee instant fixes and simple and easy outcomes: Drop weight quickly, while consuming as much as you desire! Guaranteed to work!

Sure. We are overwhelmed with quick fix services these days. And the more quick fix services there are, the more difficult it is to discover one that truly works. Lots of people have actually quit the fight loosing their bad habits as there seems no cure for them, as these supposed "quick fix" programs don't work.

Developing brand-new concerns

Can individuals truly alter their bad habits? Is it even possible to stop yourself from doing bad routines? Can you really change yourself? The response to each of these is a guaranteed "yes." However, do not anticipate changing in 24 hr, as assured by some self-help books and programs.

According to my research, and my own experience and sound judgment, anybody can change their habits, however I realise that individuals require a sincere and strong will, to be able to make a life long change.

I believe that bad options and bad practices are what brought Peter to this point-- day after day and every year-- till he struck rock bottom. That is how it work. Knowing how to totally free yourself from bad routines begins with the realisation that we trigger our own behaviour. I am the reason for my own issues.

The minute I comprehend that basic truth, I'm all set to enter the process of self-change that will result in freedom from the practices that kept me from living a more rewarding life.

Small changes are easy to do, however, releasing yourself from self-destructive practices like smoking or overindulging needs a deep, lasting change. A bad routine resembles an iceberg. If you approach it as if it were just as big as what you can see on the surface area, you will never be able to permanently change it.

You can't remove the entire thing in one day, however, if you take away a small piece everyday, you can get rid of the bad routine quicker than you believed possible. It is going to take effort on your part.

Peter believes that he can not go to the shelter, for doing so, would imply that he may miss his trip to El Paso. That is how individuals get caught up in their own spoken cages of their own making. Peter's example is a severe case, however I believe that Peter's case makes it simpler to see the genuine problems, and obstacles dealt with by individuals every day.

Peter conceals reality from himself, same as many of us do. To release ourselves from bad routines, we need to stop concealing the truth of the situation from ourselves. Overeaters, cigarette smokers, and persistent procrastinators have more in typical with individuals like Peter than it seems. All of us go to great lengths to conceal the truth from ourselves about the harmful nature of our bad routines.

Do self help programs work? Countless cigarette smokers have actually stopped permanently without following a treatment program. On the other hand, many individuals who attempt a smoking-cessation program are unable to stop, no matter the number of various programs they attempt. Some research study recommends that for each individual who stops smoking cigarettes by following a treatment program, there are nearly twenty individuals who stop by themselves.

What conclusion should we draw from all of this? It's quite clear, I believe. You have a much better change of releasing yourself from a bad routine by becoming your own coach, by taking responsibility for your own program.

The objective of this study is to offer you the technique that will empower you to free yourself from bad practices. Countless individuals have actually been successful in breaking a bad routine, therefore can you.

"Bad" Practices vs. "Good" Practices

Normally, bad practices start innocently. Due to the fact that my college roomie smoked and I was curious about what it felt and tasted like, I smoked my very first cigarette. However, bad practices tend to rapidly snowball.

A single bad practice can function as a magnet to others. Individuals who smoke typically tend to consume too much alcohol. Individuals who drink too much, often hang out at gambling establishments. Individuals who gamble may be likely to pick up woman off the streets, or consume drugs.

Quickly, something that started as a peculiarity or a one-off has actually intensified into a way of life that is self-destructive, damages your reputation and eventually can destroy your profession, your family, your health and even end your life.

Examples of Bad Practices

Virtually any practice that can be thought as "good" can have a "bad" equivalent:

- Damaging individual routines like cigarette smoking, drinking and abusing drugs
- Overindulging or not living a healthy way of life
- Making bad monetary choices
- Betting
- Hesitating
- Being addicted to sex or porn

Anything that disrupts your capability to live a healthy and happy life can be thought as a bad practice.

When Is a Bad Practice Truly A Dependency?

Individuals who are addicted to drugs, alcohol, sex, betting or other self-destructive behaviours, often say that the physical and mental dependency prevents them from conquering these bad habits.

However you do not require to have a chemical or mental dependency to have a dependency. Dependency is specified as "The state of being shackled to a routine or practice ... to such a level that its cessation triggers extreme injury." So, in truth, any bad practice is a dependency due to the fact that it oppresses us, avoiding us from attaining our greatest capacity.

Make no error: There will be repercussions for reversing any bad practice. Yet these are absolutely nothing to fear. Discomfort is short-lived; giving up lasts permanently.

Our Need for Habitual Behaviour, Beliefs and routines.

Routines are not just helpful, we really depend on our daily routines to cope in our every day lives. Physiologists inform us that of the 11,000 signals we get from our senses, our brain just knowingly processes about 40. So our brains utilise the familiarity of practices so that we can concentrate on other "greater worth" activities.

Things like strolling, chewing our food, and talking do not need the sort of psychological focus that fixing mathematics issues or playing computer game do. These activities are carried out without any mindful intent.

Social practices work the exact same method. Many people will shower at the very same time every day or constantly drive the exact same path to work. These practices are carried out basically without mindful idea.

Unfavourable practices - like overindulging, smoking cigarettes or driving to quick - work the exact same method. We seldom think of these things, even when they are putting us in risk or harmful our health or well- being.

Utilising Practices to Attain Success.

Often, we are unable to even know that we have bad practices. Have you ever dealt with someone who has bad health, or had a pal who consumed to much alcohol? Normally, those individuals do not knowingly choose to perform their bad routine. They simply do it out of ... well, routine!

When we put in the time to identify our own bad practices, take restorative action and change them with healthy and favourable ones, the outcome is an irreversible modification that pays dividends to our health, success, and joy, for the rest of our lives.

Envision being a fit and healthy person who exercise daily, without even considering it. Or somebody who constantly makes the best healthy food choices, Isn't that something that is preferable? If you could make healthy, favourable decisions all the time without even thinking of it, your life would be much easier, or would't it?

When you can change your bad practices with really good ones, you can likewise remove the tension and stress, and anxiety that those bad practices triggered in your life, so that you can at last attain the feeling of success, joy and wellness that you have actually constantly wanted.

Breaking your bad practices and changing them with good ones can assist you to accomplish that joy.

Are you all set to begin?

ONE

It Takes 21 Days to Change a Habit

You are embarking on a journey that is literally going to change the way you live. The rewards you enjoy will be massive and lifelong, once you accept the way how to transform your bad routine or habits into good ones.

IT DOESN'T MATTER how long you have actually had your bad routines. They could be something you have done since your youth, such as lying or biting your fingernails. As long as you can identify that the habit you doing is damaging, and genuinely wish to transform it into something favourable, you can change any of your bad ways into good ones.

CHANGING Habits

EVERYONE HAS bad things they are doing. If it's the Pope, George Clooney, the Dalai Lama or the Archbishop of Canterbury, people are human, they sometimes make mistakes, and these errors can frequently become bad habits. You genuinely can do anything you put your mind to. The human will is strong and the changes which lie ahead are going to surprise and amaze you. All it will take, is the will to do it.

WHAT'S SO Unique about 21 Days? You might have heard that it takes 21 days to alter a habit or routine. That's one reason domestic rehab centres for drug and alcohol abuse normally last 21 days. It takes that long for the body to eliminate the poisonous substances that it is addicted to. But it's also how long it considers the mind to expel the poisonous unfavourable ideas, that trigger it to hold on to bad practices, so that they can replace them with positive ones.

THREE WEEKS or a month likewise is an excellent timeframe to work with, when changing habits because it corresponds with our calendar system. If you target the first day of the month for the beginning of a routine modification, then it's easy to use that month as a structure to deal with your goal (" I'm going to get this done by Week 2, that done by Week 2 ..." and so on).

NOT EVERY BAD routine requires 21 days or a month to alter. Some can take longer and some can take less time. For instance, if your objective is to get out of bed a half hour earlier every day so you can make your mornings more productive, you most likely can make this a habit within a week to 10 days.

BUT ROUTINES that go deeper into your character - such as being kinder to your partner, or becoming a more spiritually centred individual, or losing the additional weight that is making you overweight and out of shape, and changing it with muscle - can take months and even years to achieve fully.

. . .

EVERYONE HAS EXPERIENCED the frustration of helplessness that come with having bad habits. When you are doing something you know is bad for you, you trigger a psychic hurt that can impact your self-esteem (" I should be a bad person because I always (Insert Bad Practice Here"). But at the same time, bad habits can always be overcome, as long as you are relentless and apply the right techniques, which will be detailed in detail in this study.

SOME HABITS ARE MORE severe than others. While biting your fingernails might not be particularly healthy or sanitary, it probably isn't as bad as eating fast food every day which eventually will cause a down spiral in your health.

MAKING bad choices generally results in making more bad choices. Even the most harmless decision can sometimes cause a downward spiral that leaves you wondering what simply took place. Even the smallest of bad habits can have an extensive unfavourable effect on the rest of your life.

CHEATING ON YOUR TAXES, for example, can lead to "changes" on your hourly timesheet, which can cause "borrowing" from your company's petty money fund, which can result in altering the books so that additional funds are diverted into your private accounts. You've graduated from a tax cheat into an embezzler!

THE WILL TO CHOOSE.

YOU CONSTANTLY HAVE A CHOICE, nevertheless. Even the most degenerate emaciated, drug-addled street addict or someone 400 pounds overweight with diabetes, hypertension and heart disease can decide to turn their life around. That's one of the gifts of being human. You have the capability to put and end to bad routines and convert them into good ones. And it's never ever, too late. All it requires is the will to try and being brave enough to make favourable changes in your life. That's the hard part. The rest is simple.

GOAL SETTING

WHEN YOU CROSS the Rubicon and decide to impact favourable modification in your life, all you require to do is to follow the process set out in this study and you can achieve your goals within whatever timeline you pick.

PERSONAL GOAL SETTING IS when you apply practical expectations to your desired result. In One of the future chapters, you are going to learn how to develop useful, concrete goals that you can follow.

ACCEPTING Duty

NONE of this occurs in a vacuum, nevertheless. Any bad practices you have are yours and yours alone. Blaming other people or situations for your bad habits will not do anything to assist you to conquer them.

PERHAPS YOU DID NOT HAVE accountable parents, or you were bullied in school. So what? While these things might have added to your bad habits, they aren't going to assist you to conquer them. In truth, any unwillingness to accept responsibility for your bad practices will eventually sabotage your efforts and avoid you from achieving your set goals.

HONESTY AND MATURITY are 2 key elements that separate those people who can effectively alter their lives and those who are predestined to continuo in their old ways, and repeat the very same errors over and over again.

TWO

Negativity and Positive Emotions

Many individuals do not even realise that they have bad practices. They simply wonder why the universe keeps conspiring versus them and causing them to have such awful luck. They never ever even realise that in most cases they are the cause of all of their own issues through the bad routines they keep repeating.

IN ORDER TO MAKE REAL, positive enhancements in your life, the first step is to develop self-awareness. If you aren't even aware of what your current routines are, you can't effectively choose new routines. In this chapter, we are going to stroll through the process of becoming more aware of your thoughts, sensations and actions so that you can see the connection between them, and the things that are happening in your life because of them.

BY ESTABLISHING this sense of self-awareness, you can move your subconscious thoughts and feelings into the mindful sphere of your thinking, analyse these ideas so that they can make the connection in between your bad habits and their repercussions to your life, and after that, select new behaviours based on what you discovered about yourself.

WHAT IS IT YOU WANT?

EVERYONE WANTS something out of life. For some, it may be a delighted, fulfilling marriage. For others, it's unlimited wealth and power. For others, it could be spiritual knowledge or a feeling of nearness to a greater power.

WHAT IS it you desire more than anything else out of life? Attempt to believe in "broad view" terms. Rather than simply wishing to stop cigarette smoking, your objective might be to achieve optimum health. Rather than simply to settle a staggering amount of financial obligation, consider your objective as taking pleasure in financial security and even prosperity for the rest of your life.

PRODUCING SELF AWARENESS.

When you have determined some overriding goals - believe. The next action is to understand what has been preventing you from achieving these goals. This can be accomplished through a number of techniques, including: .

- Reflection - Think of past experiences and then use your understanding of how you behaved during those occasions so that you can apply what you gained from them to future situations.
- Pals and Family - Open lines of communication with others by asking individuals you trust if they also see your bad routine.
- Compare Yourself With Others - Consider people who

already have the good habits you desire and think about what they do differently than you when challenged to appropriate scenarios.

- Readily available Information - Are there any books, courses or videos that can assist you to attain your objective? What sort of things do you discover when you browse online?
- Start a Journal - It's almost impossible to remember each thought and advancement you have along the way. Keep a journal so you can monitor your development and refer back to what you have actually learned.

PRODUCE Quantifiable Goals - Start to think about what success will appear like. What measurable occasion needs to happen for you to believe you have successfully accomplished your objective?

THERE MAY BE MORE than one bad practice that you want to change. You might desire to prioritise and assault these one at a time. When you discover how to conquer your first bad habit, nevertheless, the other ones will be much easier to break.

KEEPING A HABIT JOURNAL.

AS SOON AS you have actually chosen a bad habit or routine that you want to break, the next step is to develop an awareness about the habit or routine. One way to do this is to keep a Habit Journal, which is simply a record of how you did out versus your goal.

FOR INSTANCE, if your goal is to stop smoking, you will want to begin monitoring the number of cigarettes you smoked daily and what time you smoked them. If you wish to stop eating way too much, make a note of everything that you eat throughout the day. If your objective is to stop telling lies, every time you lie to somebody, document what you said, who you said it too, and, if understood, why you said it.

THIS KIND of tangible details will help you better understand what you do and exactly why. Often, the results you find and the patterns you discover may surprise you.

SOURCE OF BAD Habits

AFTER YOU HAVE RECOGNISED a bad habit and begun to track it in your life, this will often result in searching for the root causes of your bad routine. While you don't want to blame other individuals for your bad routines - you own them, they are totally yours alone - you can still attempt to understand what is triggering these bad routines.

FOR INSTANCE, if your bad habit is that you use rough language too often, pay attention to when you find yourself swearing. Who are you with? Who do you never swear in front of? Or if your bad practice is that you are a compulsive gambler, what are the triggers that get you thinking about gambling? Do you have to go by a casino or racetrack on your way home from work every day?

COMPREHENDING the circumstances and triggers that trigger us to act on our bad habits are a very important finding to help us getting rid of them later.

· · ·

CONSEQUENCES

THE NEXT STEP in getting to know your bad habit is something I like to call "Putting 2 and 2 together". Earlier, you considered what it was you desired out of life. You identified some global objectives that you wanted to work toward. Maybe you were able to picture an idealised life for your self or there is somebody you appreciate who is living the type of life you want on your own.

NOW I DESIRE you to consider what is it that is preventing you from attaining this ideal situation. What is it about your bad routine that is standing in the way of you and your objective? In other words, I desire you to "do the mathematics" so that you can see exactly how your actions are directly causing the repercussion that you are experiencing.

IT IS SIMPLY A DOMINO EFFECT. Your bad habits are the cause. The impact is that you aren't living the life you want. Yet for your entire life up to this point, you have not had the ability to put 2 and two together and pertain to the realisation that your actions are triggering your repercussions.
Until now!

MAKING a Commitment to Yourself So far, so good. You've identified something about yourself that you wish to change, you have actually engaged in the process of self-awareness and it has resulted in the understanding that the actions that you personally are taking are the cause of the repercussions you are experiencing.

WHAT REMAINS IS for you to make a durable and individual commitment to changing those actions so that you can alter those consequences. I'm not talking about merely stating some magic words or making another empty guarantee. What's needed is for you to make a permanent and solemn dedication - a contract with yourself, if you choose - that obligates you to achieving your goal.

IT PROBABLY HAS ACTUALLY TAKEN you years, if not a lifetime, to get to where you are today. Simply assuring to yourself that you are going to change right now is about as reliable as spitting into the wind. Rather, spend some time to think of what it is you want. Consider why it is very important that you succeed. How will your life be different, when you have broken your bad habit? What will be the effects if you continue to take part in the bad behaviour?

REASONS AND INNER Discussion

AS SOON AS you have actually made up your mind and are committed to making positive modifications in your life (which will not take place right now or all at once ... This is a process), the next step is to stop making reasons or allowing negative inner discussion to affect your choice making.

YOU ALREADY HAVE ADMITTED the truth that you are solely accountable for your behaviour. It's not your environment, how you were raised, or how other people have treated you. These are the kinds of reasons and negativity that people use as a crutch in order to justify their bad habits. When you have actually made an authentic decision to change, they no longer have any power over you.

START PAYING attention to what you are thinking right before and throughout the bad habit you wish to break. What excuses do you automatically bring up? What type of rationality do you utilise that enables you to do whatever it is you want to stop doing? These are the feelings and ideas you will need to get rid of.

THREE

Good Habits Is A Game Changer

Congratulations! The hardest part is over. Increasing your self-awareness to the point where you realise that you have to make a change is the hardest part of the self-improvement procedure. Unlike 99.99% of individuals with bad habits, you are now able to admit you have a problem and accept full responsibility for dealing with it.

THE LAST CHAPTER was the most challenging part of change. It's natural for individuals not to want to admit a weak point or to deny they have an issue that requires to be dealt with. Yet making this breakthrough is an essential part of the recovery process. And you have made it!

NOW, it is time to turn our attention to developing an environment of positivity that is going to provide you the strength and the support you need to nurture yourself to a brand-new life-affirming habit.

• • •

BENEFITS OF GOOD Routines

YOU MIGHT REMEMBER that about 95% of the things we do every day are out of routine. When you can change and get rid of bad habits and change them with good ones, positive things will begin to happen to you instantly.

LEGENDARY MOTIVATIONAL SPEAKER Earl Nightingale said that if you dedicate just one hour daily to studying within your field, you can get to a management position within your chosen profession in simply 3 years. One hour per day of research study will make you a nationwide authority in five years. And within 7 years, you can be among the most recognised professionals worldwide.

CHECKING out an hour each day in your field equates to about one book per week. So you can see that something as simple as developing a favourable routine like reading for a hour per day can not only bring positivity, it can actually transform your life.

LIKE AN AIRLINER that has all of the substantial flight details programmed into its onboard computer so that it can fly on automatic pilot, the excellent practices we develop are the "mental software" that will permit us to reach our ultimate objectives without even needing to think about it.

STEP 1 - DISCOVERING YOUR PURPOSE. To discover your purpose in life, ask yourself these questions:

- Who am I?
- Why am I here?
- What do I want to achieve with my life?

- What would make me feel most satisfied?
- What do I value more than anything?
- Do I believe in God, a higher power, or the will of the universe?
- How does this affect the options I make?

STEP 2 - DEVELOPING Your Vision Statement

Think of the answers to the above questions. Write them down someplace and try to organise them so that there is some sort of order or pattern. This is how you specify your belief system, which is the overriding function behind your life.

IF YOU CAN'T SEE the pattern right now, try to assess these additional concerns:

- How would I pick to live if I could do anything on the planet?
- If you never ever had to stress over cash once again, how would you spend your days and night?
- At the end of your life, what will you point to as your essential accomplishment?
- What would you like people to say about you at your funeral service?

ARE you beginning to see it now? What you are discovering is your vision of how you desire your life to be. The next action is to arrange that vision into a single sentence or paragraph - called a Vision Statement-- that specifies what you desire out of life.

HERE IS an example of a vision statement:

" I am a homemaker and also working, I want to live my best family and working life - both. I want to end up being a successful human. I want to improve my character, and likewise the growth of the company and myself. I want to earn money to make my household and society a better place."

WHAT DOES your Vision Declaration look like?

STEP 3: STRUCTURE Your Power Goals

Your Vision Statement is where you wish to go. Your power goals are how you prepare to get there. To develop these power goals, let's return for a minute to the bad routine that you recognised that you want to break. Think about how this bad habit impacts you in each of these locations of your life: Spiritual, Work or Career, Personal Development, Health, Relationships, Money, Friends or Social Life, Family Life.

NOT EVERY BAD routine will have an effect on every element of your life, however you may be surprised on how deeply harmful your bad practices can be. To establish your power goals, just finish the connection between how breaking your bad habit will cause an improvement in each particular area that you have recognised.

FOR INSTANCE, let's presume the bad routine you wish to break is that you are addicted to betting:

- Health: Your addiction to gambling causes you to lose sight of what is very important in life, end up being anti-social, end up being financial unsteady and most likely end up in a financial obligation.
- Power Goal: When you break the bad practice of gaming, you will end up being more positive in life,

> develop favourable objectives and stop squandering money (in the end the house always wins).
> - Relationships: Gambling takes a toll on your relationships and financial situation.
> - Power Goal: Once you are made with gaming, you will work to reconnect with your good friends, family, partner and enhance your financial situation.

CONTINUE with this workout with each category right down the line. If there is no direct correlation between your bad habit and a specific area of your life, simply avoid it and go to the next one.

WHY GOALS ARE Necessary for Joy?

WHEN YOU COMPILE a list of Power Objectives, they will provide the structure upon which you will construct your strategy for attaining your vision declaration. When this journey has actually been broken down into smaller attainable actions, you will have the ability to not just break your bad habits, but you will live your life on autopilot.

AS LONG AS you follow your plan regularly and constantly, your long-term success is practically guaranteed. Obviously, things can still go wrong and life will continue to throw the occasional curve ball at you. However due to the fact that you have had the ability to break a bad habit and replace it with a good one-- and duplicate the process over and over once again until all of your bad practices are in your past - you will have the strength and personal determination to conquer any setback.

· · ·

RESEARCHING YOUR PATH.

WHEN IT CONCERNS ACCOMPLISHING your power goals, understanding is power. The more details you have about your goal, and about how other individuals have accomplished it, the more tools you will have at your disposal when it comes time to act upon your objectives.

HANG around on the Internet researching whatever you can about your objectives. Look particularly for blog sites and online forums that are related to your specific bad routine. Provided the size and scope of the web, there will definitely be numerous websites that are particularly devoted to any particular issue. You make sure to find a wealth of information and motivating individual stories that will help encourage you.

Stop Playing for Time and Get More Done Faster

The second hardest part is staying focused on your goals, if the hardest part about altering a bad habit into a good one is admitting that you have a problem. Life has a tendency to obstruct of our objectives and it's easy to end up being side-tracked or fall back into our old behaviours.

IT'S ALSO EXTREMELY easy to say that you want to change something, but you continually postpone acting on what you have said. This type of procrastination can include months or perhaps years before you accomplished your objective. It may even thwart your habit-breaking procedure entirely.

THE EFFECTS of Procrastination

PROCRASTINATION IS JUST one more thing that individuals use to prevent doing the effort of attaining their goals. In the very same way that no one else is responsible for your bad habits - you own them and it depends on you to fix them - postponing the unavoidable is just another way of shirking responsibility.

WHEN YOU PUT things off (" I'll start next week" or "I'm not all set yet"), you are only cheating yourself. You may have all idea to alter your life, however, without direct action, you will never attain the goals you have set.

POWER GOALS

OFTEN, procrastination is a problem because individuals overthink all the huge problems rather than break them down into smaller sized, more manageable actions. It's like the old saying goes: How do you consume an elephant? One bite at a time!

WHEN YOU BELIEVE, "Oh, my goodness, I need to stop consuming" or "I can't believe I have a lot of financial obligation to settle" or whatever your bad routine, it can be daunting. However, by breaking your goals into a series of much easier steps and organising them into a timed sequence of events, you can impact positive deeds without having to slay all of your negative habits simultaneously.

INSPIRATION AND INTEREST

IT'S useful to have the inspiration to keep you on course. This can be either internal or external motivation. Internal motivation is things you do to support your decision to make modifications in your life, such as putting up inspirational messages in places where you will see them regularly or giving yourself incentives for favourable behaviour.

. . .

BE IMAGINATIVE. For example, if your goal is to drop weight, find an image of yourself at your fattest, have it blown up and tape it to the door of your refrigerator. When you sneak into the cooking area for a late night snack, this will trigger you to definitely think twice.

EXTERNAL MOTIVATION IS when other people encourage and support you to success. These can be friends, family, and professionals like therapists and life coaches, and even specialists who have actually composed books or produced videos that inspire you.

THE MORE EXTERNAL and internal inspiration you utilise to keep you on your chosen path, the more passionate you will end up being about your journey and the more likely you will be to prosper and attain your Power Goals.

INTERRUPTING Negative Behaviour

UNDOUBTEDLY, there will be problems. Nobody is made perfect and you will occasionally fail or succumb to temptation. It is possible, however, to short circuit this bad behaviour by attempting to interrupt negative behaviour as quickly as you recognise the triggers associated with your bad habit.

WHILE YOU WERE DEVELOPING the self-awareness that caused the recognition of your bad habits, you identified a series of triggers or patterns that normally preceded your acting on your bad habits. These can be ideas you have or physical sensations like sights or smells that lure you.

. . .

TYPICALLY, merely avoiding these kinds of triggers is enough to keep you on track. However if you accidentally or unknowingly trip into one of these triggers, you can interrupt your possible negative behaviour by removing yourself from that circumstance. Drop everything and go in the opposite direction.

FOR INSTANCE, if your bad routine is alcoholism and you expect just encounter an old "drinking buddy", consider a reason to avoid that individual as rapidly as possible. The longer you spend with that individual, the greater the possibilities that your desire to have a drink will be activated.

KEEPING CONCENTRATED On the Benefits of Good Habits. Conquering temptations can be difficult, particularly at the start line of your journey to break your bad habits. One efficient manner in which can help you is to remind yourself of why you wish to break the habit in the very first place.

EARLIER, you identified the advantages of replacing your bad habit or routine with a good one. These benefits were boiled down into your personal Vision Declaration. Keep this handy so that you can revisit it whenever you require to. Keep a copy of your Vision Statement in your wallet or purse so that you can pull it out and read it when you end up being lured to go back to your earlier bad behaviour.

TYPICALLY, merely advising yourself of what you desire out of life and how avoiding temptation in the moment will help you accomplish your objective in the long term is enough to give you the strength to make better options.

. . .

BENEFIT AND PENALTY

CONDITIONING IS a term utilised in psychology to describe the process of how benefit and punishment impacts behaviour. Conditioning also applies to real life. You work at your job because you are rewarded with a paycheque. You pay your taxes, because you wish to prevent the punishment of going to jail for tax evasion.

WHEN BREAKING A BAD ROUTINE, using little rewards to reinforce favourable behaviour is an exceptional method to keep you encouraged and engaged in the bad habit breaking process.

IF, for example, your objective is to lose 30 pounds within 6 months, integrate in a benefit structure that enhances your hitting various turning points: Buying yourself a new attire every time you lose 5 pounds or treat yourself to a spa treatment when you reach the middle.

THE PENALTY, however, is less effective due to the fact that some people will determine a method to exploit a punishment structure in order to "authorise" unwanted behaviour. Not much tends to get success under this method.

FOR EXAMPLE, if your bad practice is swearing and you create a penalty structure in which you have to pay $1 into a piggy bank each time you use a curse word, you may find yourself conserving up your money so that you can curse at will. Simply put, the penalty becomes "worth it" in order to perform the bad habit. This is not a favourable method to try breaking a bad habit.

. . .

PUNISHMENT LIKEWISE SUSTAINS unfavourable thoughts with your bad habit. When you penalise yourself, it adversely impacts your self-esteem: "I'm such a horrible person that I should have to be punished". The idea is to develop positivity and optimism, not reinforce poor self-image and pessimism. So when it comes to breaking bad habits or routines, utilise a lot of carrots but keep away from the stick!

ELIMINATING NEGATIVITY

YOU WILL BE MORE likely to achieve your Power Objectives if you eliminate as much negativeness from your life as possible. This consists of both internal and external negativity. Internal negativity includes feelings and ideas you have about yourself that are damaging to your self-confidence. When these types of emotions and thoughts begin to creep up, just expel them from your mind. Through the power of will, you can choose to think favourably.

EXTERNAL NEGATIVENESS CAN BE MORE CHALLENGING to stop. These are things that other people say to you or reveal non-verbally that are crucial or damaging to your self-confidence. They include such things as painful comments from your employer, nagging from your other half, or "teasing" from your buddies. If you wish to improve your chances of accomplishing your Power Goals, it's required that you shut them down or shut them out.

IF SOMEONE HAS a negative viewpoint of you or states something mean or nasty to you, it doesn't mean that you have to listen to them. Simply shut them out by not focusing on what they are saying or letting it roll off you like water off a duck's back. Negativity is the enemy of your journey to attain your Vision Statement and, and requires to be banished from your life in whatever form it takes.

FIVE

Plan Of Action (The Game Plan)

You have established self-awareness so that you acknowledge your bad habits, made a personal commitment to replace them with good habits, established a Vision Statement to assist you to where you wish to go, and created Power Objectives that will take you there.

THE NEXT STEP is to produce a Game Plan that will break your journey down into possible steps. In my viewpoint, this is the most pleasurable part of breaking bad practices and changing them with great ones due to the fact that you get to develop the structure you will use throughout the next several days or months to turn your objectives into reality.

PREPARING Your Tactical Plan

YOUR STRATEGY IS AN ACTION STRATEGY, just like generals draw up when planning to lead their armies into a fight. It is going to be a real, tangible strategy that consists of measurements that can be observed, built-in rewards to inspire you to reach both short- and long-term goals, and has a concluding accomplishment: Living your Vision Statement every day so that you can be happy and productive.

IT STARTS with your Power Goals. Pull these out and think about how long it will realistically take for you to accomplish each of them. Don't be overly indulgent. Your Strategy should challenge you to reach your objectives as quickly as you can. The more time you permit yourself to persist with your bad practice, the harder it will be to break.

LET'S take a look at an example of what a Strategy may appear like. Assume the bad habit you wish to break is that you bet too much and that you presently go to the gambling establishment every Friday and Saturday night, buy lottery tickets daily, go to the race-track every Sunday and bet on sports a number of times each week. That's a lot of gambling!

WHEN DETERMINING YOUR POWER OBJECTIVES, the "Household" objective you set was: Household-- My dependency to gambling methods I invest a little time with my spouse and children. I also spend a big portion of my income on my betting, to the degree that there is typically not enough to buy groceries or pay my children's tuition.

POWER OBJECTIVE-- STOP GAMBLING SO that I can be home more and be encouraging of my family both emotionally and economically. In these circumstances, stopping cold turkey might not have a high portion of success. You may have attempted to stop many times previously, but always receded back into your bad practice.

RATHER, your Power Objective can be broken down into a series of steps that are possible and come with an integrated benefit structure

- By the end of Week 1, I will cut up my subscription card to the casino's VIP club, stop banking on sports, and just purchase one lottery game ticket each week. At the end of the week, with the money I save I will take my household out to dinner at a restaurant.
- By the end of Week 2, I will end my Sunday "tradition"of going to the track and will restrict my check outs to the gambling establishment to one night per week. With the cash I conserve, I will pay my children's overdue tuition.
- By the end of Week 3, I will willingly put myself on the gambling establishment's "banned clients" list and not purchase any lottery game tickets. This will end my gambling practice. As a reward, I will dedicate to prepare a minimum of one fun household activity each weekend, such as going to the zoo or going camping.

NOTICE that there is no penalty involved. Restart the clock and try once again if you don't succeed in fulfilling your commitment for the week. As long as you stay dedicated and focused, ultimately you will make a move and get it done with.

ASKING for Help

. . .

SOME BAD HABITS are very difficult to conquer them by yourself. Dependencies to drugs, alcohol, gaming, sex and other deadly habits might need you to get expert assistance, along with the support of your family and friends.

IT'S natural not to want to ask for help. People's natural pride makes it not easy to do. However if your bad habit is so strong that you aren't going to be able to break it without help, then you require to set your reluctance aside and rely on other individuals to assist you.

CONSIDER IT BY DOING THIS: There is no shame in wanting to be a better person. Although it might seem to you that other people may believe less of you if you admit that you have a problem, in reality many people are going to offer you credit for attempting to do something about it.

MILESTONES AND TIMELINES

FOR THE MOST PART, it takes 21 days or a month to break a bad habit. It's handy, although not vital, that you start your Game Plan on the very first day of a brand-new month. This simply makes it much easier to set up the timelines and milestones you will need to ease yourself into your new positive behaviour patterns. If possible if you can't wait up until the start of a new month then at least wait up until the beginning of the new week.

WHEN YOU ARE DEVELOPING your Game Plan, do not simply take it a week at a time. To put it simply, do not just plan the first week's goals and see how it goes from there. To enhance your opportunities of success, plan out the whole Tactical plan over several weeks up until you reach your supreme Power Goal.

. . .

WHEN WRITING YOUR GAME PLAN, every brand-new week must grow on the success of the week before - so that by the end, you have totally removed the bad routine you wanted to break, and replaced it with a great habit that will improve the quality of your life, and push you towards accomplishing your Vision Statement.

HANDLING Obstacles

KNOW AHEAD of time that you are going to experience problems. The secret is to not to let failure hinder the entire process. Among the benefits of having a Game Plan is that if you stop working to reach a specific week's objectives, you don't have to start over from the start. You can simply restart that particular week and move everything up a week.

MAYBE YOU WERE MOVING TOO quick or didn't realise how much time you required to accomplish a specific action in your journey. Go back and repeat the step till you get it right. Only then should you move on to the next step.

REMAINING POSITIVE

IT'S critical that you not let your setbacks cause you to fall back into a negative attitude. Errors are going to be made. We are only human. Accept that you are imperfect and move on. However, do not dwell on the fact that you have started over, or consider yourself as a failure.

. . .

THE EXTREMELY TRUTH that you are trying to make your life much better suggests that you are the reverse of a failure. If you do not be successful all the time-- and you will not-- you can still be successful. The most essential thing is to stay positive and to just keep attempting. As long as you are making the effort to get better, you are a winner.

SIX

Blueprint for Successful Habit Formation

To be able to learn a brand-new routine, we ought to actually teach ourselves to do that habit over and over till we do it automatic, without even considering it.

MAKING Use Of Reminders

A USEFUL METHOD TO get yourself to keep focus is using reminders. These can be post-It notes, emails, text messages and voicemails you can send out to yourself so that you are bombarded with constant pointers that will keep you motivated and concentrated on your goal.

THE POWER of Routine

THE VERY SAME thing that is done at the very same time every day, becomes a ritualised experience. For instance, if you have an "early morning routine" of taking a shower, drinking some coffee, using the bathroom, getting dressed and preparing yourself for work, you most of the time follow the very same specific very same regular every day without even thinking of it.

THIS SAME KIND of routine can be used to your new routines. Perform the very same actions at the very same time and series every day up until second nature. That method you will acquire the advantages of your good habits without thinking to do them.

SECRETS TO CONSISTENCY

SOMETHING IS a routine if it doesn't need any thought on your part. Try to ensure your new good routine is carried out consistently by repeating it every day for 21 days to 1 month. When you keep doing the very same thing over and over at the same time and location and in the very same way, you will start to regularly follow your new great routine as second nature.

SEVEN

The Six Stages In the Process Of Self-Change

Change is not an event, but a journey. Change happens through a series of phases, and most successful people have failed a few times before they succeed. Self-control alone will not do it.

You require to understand the cycle of modification, or you risk substituting one bad practice for another, as so frequently happens when ex- smokers please their craving for "something" by overeating. Success depends on having the right information and knowing how to utilise it.

SCIENTISTS HAVE IDENTIFIED six clear phases in the process of effective self-change:

    1. Rejection
    2. Realisation
    3. Preparation
    4. Action
    5. Upkeep
    6. Termination

. . .

FOR MOST PEOPLE, the process of breaking a bad habit or routine is not a straight path that takes them from one stage to the next. Effective self-changers typically follow a path that's more like a spiral: They progress, return to a previous phase, and proceed to the next level of dedication one or more times before breaking the routine permanently.

QUITTING a routine like cold turkey normally does not work. If a person isn't ready to continue, pressing her into the action stage will trigger her to feel like a failure the first time she make a mistake. She may end up more addicted to her habit than she was prior to she tried to stop. If she feels guilty and blames herself for stopping working to break the habit, she will discover its even harder to make a dedication to stop the next time.

WHATEVER YOUR BAD HABIT IS, you might have tried to break it many times, too. This time will be different, because you'll understand that breaking your habit is a process, not an occasion. You will have the confidence and the knowledge to prosper this time.

Stage 1 Rejection

Removing the Blinders

At the age of 72, Jason is a persistent complainer. I discovered a long period of time ago that I do not need to purchase a newspaper or watch television to understand what's wrong with the world; there are plenty of individuals like Jason who will tell me what's wrong. Complaining, gossiping, criticising, and negative attitude are a few of the most dangerous habits.

Bit by bit, negativity gnaws at a person's health and eliminates the possibility for happiness. If somebody close to you is a a criticiser, or a negative thinker, your own wellness is at danger.

Complaining about things beyond our direct control is among the most destructive habits. Yes, I know, it's likewise one of the most typical things that individuals do. We grumble about the weather; we discuss whoever is the focus of the most recent celebrity scandal; we blame the federal government-- any federal government-- for everything that's wrong.

Grumbling about things we can't control is a very reliable method to prevent confronting things that we can do something about. By spending his life complaining about things that he is helpless to change, Jason prevents needing to confront his own negative attitude and bitterness.

Jason desires everybody else to change. He blames everyone else for his problems: his mom and dad, a former business partner, the government, the local economy. In his present state, he can't accept that his misery has nothing to do with any of these things, but have to do with his habit of blaming others for what's wrong in his life.

Jason doesn't have bad habits that causes a clear health danger. He doesn't smoke, drink alcohol, use drugs, or overeat. But his health spiralled downwards, and he is fretted about the need for a major surgery. Although negative thinking hasn't been conclusively linked to cancer or heart disease, scientists are starting to discover proof that bitterness, hatred, and animosity literally kills people. Jason feels no factor to change his own mindset or behaviour.

Jason is a traditional example of a person who is not able to recognise the true reason for his distress. Jason is in denial. Denial is the first stage in the cycle of self-change. The huge bulk of individuals whose health, happiness, or relationships are being threatened by a self-destructive routine spend months, if not years, in a stage where they deny the seriousness of the problem.

Individuals in this phase share the following qualities:

- They do not accept that they have a major issue.
- They withstand change and typically become aggressive if faced about the need to alter.
- They have a basic sense of hopelessness, no matter how busy their lives appear to be on the surface.
- Many individuals who have self-destructive habits likewise experience a feeling of of distress. According to

research, approximately 50% of drug users have some kind of depression.

Lots of people are so fixated in their unconscious need to defend their bad habits that they refuse help even when their lives depend on it.

People usually need an unexpected response prior to they can remove the blinders. This is a fact that hasn't altered in the last 3,000 years, as the following story illustrates. King David was among the heroes of ancient Israel. He was the leader of his nation, a terrific warrior, an accomplished musician, and one of the best poets of antiquity.

When he was a young shepherd tending his father's flock, he killed a bear and a lion with his hands. He eliminated Goliath on the battleground when he was barely a teenager. One evening, the king got out of bed and went up to the roofing of his house. He saw a beautiful female cleaning herself nearby. Right away he sent his servant to discover who she was. Her name was Bathsheba. She was the other half of a soldier called Uriah, who was one of Israel's bravest and most faithful soldiers. Uriah was away from home, serving his nation in a war versus one of Israel's numerous enemies.

David sent for Bathsheba and slept with her. She became pregnant. The king desired Uriah out of the way. The Israeli army was besieging an opponent city at the time. David sent out a letter to the leader of his army, Joab, in which he laid out directions for eliminating Uriah. He told Joab to send out Uriah to the front of the battle, then retreat with the rest of his soldiers, leaving Uriah alone.

Joab carried out the king's orders and Uriah was eliminated in battle. David made Bathsheba his wife, and she provided him a son.

There are a great deal of things going on here that are even worse than smoking, overspending, negative attitude, and overindulging--

treachery and murder, to call simply. And it began with David's lust, a nasty thing in itself. How do you inform a king that he's developing some dangerous habits?

If you think it's tough to get somebody in your own household to remove the blinders, picture what the prophet Nathan was up against. Nathan understood what was going on. As a prophet, it was his job to help the king open his eyes. Nathan didn't challenge David. Rather, he told the king a story about 2 males who lived in the exact same city.

One guy was abundant, the other poor. The rich man had numerous flocks and herds. The only thing the pauper had was one lamb. The pauper loved the lamb as if it were his child. One night the rich man needed a lamb for a supper celebration. Instead of compromising a lamb from one of his own flocks, he took the poor man's lamb. When King David heard this, he was furious-- he thought Nathan was telling him a real story about 2 males in his kingdom.

"The man who did this thing will surely die," said the king. Then Nathan stated to David, "You are the man." David listened to Nathan's story, and it opened his eyes. Why can't we listen better? Why can't we see the faults in ourselves that others see so plainly in us? It is so simple to understand when others are in denial, and virtually difficult to admit that we remain in this phase.

In the language of modern therapy, the prophet Nathan was in an assisting relationship with King David. He faced David, but not through an act of direct verbal aggression. He created uncertainty in David by reacting in a manner that David least expected. That is what allowed David to open his eyes.

Uncertainty is what causes us to search for new alternatives. Nathan understood that it's impossible to change another individual, but you can inspire him to wish to change himself. Your role as a helper is to support another person throughout the process of self-change, not to attack him or decline him.

We can't all be as smart as Nathan. But there is always a method to assist somebody open his eyes without participating in an aggressive conflict, which typically triggers permanent damage to everyone included. You are currently geared up to be a better helper by having actually read this if somebody close to you is in denial. Do not go along with him, do not cave in to him, and by all means, don't face him honestly.

If you've become aware of the need to rid yourself from a bad habit, you're currently in phase 2.

Stage 2 Realisation

When You Know You Have an Issue

Individuals in this stage know they have an issue and want to understand their problem, however they don't know what to do or they feel powerless to change. Individuals in phase 2 are still far from making a dedication to change.

Lots of people get stuck in this phase. They spend years telling themselves that they are going to change "one day." Worry of failure keeps lots of people stuck in this stage. They conceal from the reality by informing themselves that they're waiting for the "best" weight-loss program, the perfect cigarette smoking cessation program, or the best time to stop drinking.

"I'll change when the time is right," is among the phrases you hear most often from people in this stage of the self-change cycle. There will never be a "correct time," obviously, but they haven't been able to break out of their verbal cage. Some people in this stage are never ever able to make a serious commitment to alter, despite the fact that their life depends on it. We arc all familiar with the everyday experiences and struggles of ordinary individuals who are stuck in this stage.

If you are in a position to assist somebody who remains in phase 2 of the cycle, constantly keep the following points in mind:

- People in this stage require support, listening, and feedback.
- Do not offer recommendations unless you're asked for it.
- People in this phase normally need to be jolted into action, but that doesn't suggest you're the one who must apply the pressure. Attempting to press a person to take action prior to she is prepared to change can be a big mistake. Pressure at this moment will just make the person more resistant to alter. Individuals who are stuck in stage 2 really do know much better, however they have actually forgotten what they understand. Too often, an individual catastrophe needs to take place before an individual in this phase has the ability to move on.

For many individuals, there is a certain comfort in thinking that they can't avoid the devastating path they're following, despite the fact that they know where it leads in the end. They are locked into a self-defeating frame of mind that states, "I understand I'm doomed, however what can I do about it?" The answer is that they can do a lot about it, but not till they have the ability to translucent the mind video games they play.

Why do we play these games, even when we know our practices are destroying us? I believe the response goes something like this: As soon as we break out of the cage we have actually been concealing in, we will need to confess that we had the power to do all of it along. That can be a scary thing.

An individual who frees himself from a habit that has actually controlled his life for years or years can be terrified of the possibility of having to confess that he squandered a big part of his life by failing to take responsibility for his own behaviour.

A person's capability to shift her thoughts from the past to the present is the key to moving from stage 2 to stage 3. You can't make the decision to alter as long as you're still focused on the past.

As quickly as you choose to change, you're at completion of stage 2. The next action in the cycle of freeing yourself from a bad practice is the preparation phase.

Stage 3 Preparation

Planning Your Personal D-Day

We reside in a world that is accustomed to 30-second commercials that provide instantaneous solutions. But we shouldn't be amazed when the easy options do not work: There are no magic bullets, no easy solutions on the path to deep and lasting modification.

In this stage, you work on making change your number one priority. You can't move into phase 4 up until freeing yourself from the habit becomes your greatest concern. Your thoughts hold you back by triggering you to relive events over and over when you focus on the past.

Blaming ourselves for things that failed in the past is the most self-destructive routine of all. It's simple for our families and friends to see when a habit like drinking, overindulging, or over costs is destroying our lives. But it isn't always so simple, not even for individuals closest to us, to know when regret and self-blame are ruining our possibility for happiness.

The only option is to accept responsibility on your own, to realise that you can decide to organise your life. One of the keys to successful self-change is to develop your own strategy. The crucial element in any program is the self-confidence of the individual who is using it. If you think the program will work, you have a much better chance of making it work. The best method to do that is to produce your own strategy.

Beware of procrastination

The greatest threat in this phase is procrastination. Attempt these techniques at the first sign that you're trying to delay your dedication:

- Weigh the benefits of acting versus the results of procrastinating
- Set achievable objectives. Trying to pay off your credit card next month will just set you up for failure. Settling the credit card in six months or one year gives you a much higher expectation of success.
- Get going. Do something. Register for a workout class or choose a flight on your bike. Activity is the best antidote for procrastination.
- Don't beat yourself up if you're not on your best all the time. It's not about perfection-- it has to do with making progress one step at a time.

Knowing yourself is crucial to effective planning. What are the real reasons for the routines you have? What are the genuine reasons for your procrastination? Your biggest opponent at this phase is worry of failure. That's typical. Do not let it bother you. Just set a date and stick to it.

Stage 4 Action

Attacking the Problem

Remember that action isn't the first or the last action in change. To get this far, you had to alter your awareness, your emotions, and your self-image as you moved from each of the earlier stages to the next.

The objective in this phase is to alter your way of thinking. You do this by:

- Learning how to unwind when temptations are strong
- Starting a workout program
- Knowing effective "countering" strategies-- thoughts and actions that keep you from falling into your old patterns

How to defeat daily temptations

Counter acting is one of the most effective techniques in the cycle of self-change. It's much easier to promote the new behaviour than to eliminate the old one. As long as you're concentrating on trying to break the old routine, you resemble a soldier who is combating with one hand connected behind his back. Rather concentrate on your brand-new behaviour is like releasing the hand connected behind your back. Unexpectedly you have more power to bring about the modification you prefer.

People who break bad habits often experience disappointment in the early stages, when they're trying as hard as they can to remove the old behaviour.

In an extremely genuine sense, success comes when you stop trying. By focusing on your brand-new lifestyle, you stop trying to break the old habit; almost without being aware of what's occurring, you move on to the next phase as the brand-new behaviour replaces the old one.

You require a method to manage the daily temptations that occur in this stage. One of the tricks to success is to stay active. Our bodies are developed to move. But you can't exercise or go for a walk all the time. So, how do you battle temptation when you can't exercise?

The answer is RSD: relaxation, extending, and deep breathing.

- Relaxation: When you feel the desire to return to your old routine, do something that's genuinely relaxing. Consider a beautiful day at the beach. Imagine drifting in the water with the sun on your face. You can do this in just a couple of seconds. It works each time.
- Stretching: This is a terrific strategy to make use of at the workplace. I'm not talking about a 20-minute routine (although you must stretch for at least 10 to 15 minutes every day). Anytime you feel temptation strike, battle it by stretching for a few seconds. If you have just one minute, that will defeat the temptation.
- Deep breathing: Inhale and breathe out. This method works each time. Try it today. You'll see what I suggest. By keeping you in tune with the natural rhythm of your

body, these three countering strategies advise you that you don't truly want the chocolates after all.

Reward yourself

It is very important to reward yourself during this phase. Make a contract with yourself that reward you for doing your part of the agreement. Write down the terms, a contract is more binding when it's on paper.

Your agreement might state something like:

- "For every single pound I lose, I will put (You pick the amount) into a cost savings account" (shopping account, weekend trip account, etc)
- "I will transfer (You select the quantity) into my shopping account for every thirty minutes I work out."
- "I will make a contribution to charity in the amount of (You choose the quantity) for each pound I lose."

Use your imagination. Whatever you're attempting to totally free yourself from, rewarding yourself is a powerful motivator. If you decide to make a donation to charity, your reward will be tremendous. Losing undesirable weight as you contribute cash to a charity that feeds hungry kids will give you all the inspiration you need to reach your objective.

Stage 5 Upkeep

Win the Battle

Professional therapists call this phase the maintenance stage. Now, the key is to replace the bad habit with a brand-new habit. This step is crucial to your success. If you just remove the bad habit, you're condemned to always combating the desire to return. One would gladly go back to their old life style if stuck in this stage. This phase is a real battle to prevent a regression.

Lapses along with regressions teach you that real modification costs more than you believed in terms of effort, time, and cash. My lapses taught me that I needed to make a more serious commitment to getting ready for my lifestyle change. One of the most essential things I did throughout this duration was to purchase new uniforms for my basketball group.

Putting your money where your mouth is constantly helps to keep you concentrated on the goal of a way of life change. By doing this, I was starting to think more about getting in basketball shape and less about attempting to give up smoking.

I came to understand another important thing after my lapses. Each time I lapsed, I felt disgusted. But I didn't feel guilty or beat myself up for not being strong enough to adhere to my word. There is a substantial difference.

Individuals in phase 5 haven't altered their way of life yet. They are still working on changing it. For some people, the battle can certainly go on for a lifetime; others move through this stage rapidly and totally free themselves from the issue permanently.

What triggers people to regression?

Scientists have recognised 3 primary reasons for relapses:

- Overconfidence: The ex-alcoholic who states, "I can deal with one beverage," is plainly in phase 5. As everybody in AA knows, overconfidence is the No. 1 cause of regressions among its members.
- Daily temptation: A male who is fighting a dependency to porn can not stroll into a cinema that's showing an X-rated film and ask God for the strength not to look at the screen. Individuals in phase 4 still feel lured. Success depends on getting rid of daily temptations from your life. You can't remove every temptation, obviously. That's why you need to master the countering techniques covered in stage 4.
- Regret and self-blame: Telling yourself that you aren't strong enough to break the habit sets you up for a regression. It's part of the verbal cage that individuals construct to prevent obligation for their options.

Deep change must be related to a new way of living. Research shows that a diet achieves success when it is combined with consuming much healthier foods and working out. The majority of us don't need to see research findings to believe this: We see the evidence every day in our own lives and in the lives of individuals who are close to us.

The first risk sign for a dieter typically isn't overindulging, however damaging her commitment to a new way of life. She stops going to her exercise class. When she beings in front of the TV instead of exercising, she's just one action far from serving herself a huge bowl of ice cream.

My experience taught me two essential lessons:
    (1) A lapse isn't constantly a relapse;
    (2) and Regret and self-blame don't help. If I had permitted myself to feel guilty when I lapsed, I probably would have dove-tailed into a total regression, and it might have taken me another five years before I was ready to make a serious dedication to quit.
    It took years to establish your bad practice. You're most likely setting yourself up for failure if you believe you can eliminate it in a couple of days or weeks.

<h1 style="text-align:center">Stage 6 Termination</h1>

Freedom

The bad habit is broken forever as soon as you moved from stage 5 to stage 6. Now the bad habit is no longer a risk and it will never ever return. This stage is called termination by specialists.

I understand that termination is possible, since I was as addicted to nicotine as alcoholics are to alcohol, and I freed myself from cigarettes permanently.

Researchers do a lot of research study that suggests individuals can actually worry themselves to death. If you believe you will always have the urge to return to your old practice, you most likely would. Rather focus on your brand-new way of life and it's advantages, then you replaced unfavourable thoughts with favourable ones.

Freedom from bad routines occur when you replaced the bad practice with a positive one, a brand-new lifestyle. You will know that you are truly free of a bad habit, when you note all 3 these signs in the new you, and you can be sure that you have actually broken the old habit permanently:

- You experience an enduring and deep change in your self-image.
- You no longer should try to not do the old habit and do not feel lured in any circumstance.
- You enjoy your much healthier lifestyle and have real self-confidence in your power of option.

EIGHT

Living Confidently

One of the things many individuals aren't getting ready for, is success. Sometimes your mind can put limits on what you can accomplish. For instance, if your bad habit is that you overeat and your Power Goal is to lose 15 pounds. In 1 month, if your mind has a pessimistic outlook it's going to be more difficult for you to reach your goal. To put it simply, the mind often leads the body.

IT IS necessary that you train your mind to reject negativeness and accept positivity. It's possible to reprogram your mind so that success comes more quickly. All you need to do is to have beliefs that are supportive of your objective and your truth will line up with your beliefs.

AFFIRMATIONS

.   .   .

DISPELLING negativity from our worldview is much easier stated than done. For practically your whole life, your negative ideas have been enhanced by your bad habits. In your mind, you believe you will stop working to attain your Power Goal because you have constantly failed in the past, right? Not necessarily! There is a strategy you can utilise to eradicate negativeness from your mind and replace it with positive ideas. It's called using affirmations and declarations.

AFFIRMATIONS ARE a brief expression you duplicate to yourself a number of times a day, generally while taking a look at yourself in a mirror. They are designed to reprogram your mind to strengthen positivity and eradicate negativeness. They can consist of such phrases as: .

- "I am a powerful person."
- "I can achieve anything I set my mind too."
- "I am strong enough to do whatever I genuinely desire."
- "I am a happy individual who is worthy of success."

Affirmations can also be habit-centric:

- "I am going to be sober today."
- "I will spend my day smoke-free."
- "I am going to avoid the gambling establishment today."

By their meaning, affirmations are favourable declarations. So avoid affirmations that have the words "will not" or "not".

AFFIRMATIONS ARE a helpful method to focus the mind on the positive and they really work. Establish three or four affirmations that relate to your power objectives and speak them to yourself aloud in front of mirror 10 times each three times a day for a week.

. . .

AT THE END of that time, you will observe a modification in the way you feel about yourself. You will have more positive energy and negative ideas will have been banished from your worldview.

VISUALISATION AND POSITIVITY

ANOTHER STRATEGY TO promote positivity is to use visualisation exercises. When you set aside a little time every day to imagine what your life is going to look like once you replace our bad habits with great ones, this is. Try it out on your own by discovering a quiet location where you will not be disrupted for at least five to 10 minutes.

SIT CONVENIENTLY and close your eyes. Attempt to unwind completely. When your mind is calm, don't harp on your bad habit or its consequences, however rather picture what your every day life will appear like once you adopt your brand-new habits.

BE AS DETAILED as you possibly can. What will you appear like? What will other people state to you? What will you smell? What do you feel? What thoughts are you having? Visualisation prepare the mind for success by anticipating that success. Then, when you start to experience the positive effects of your good habits, you are less most likely to reject them with negativity. There are even some individuals who believe that it is possible to actively affect occasions by visualising them.

WHILE THERE MAY or might not be any direct connection in between the two, it's definitely true that preparing your mind for success through visualisation makes it easier for you to embrace that success once it gets here.

. . .

MAKING a Vision Board

Vision boards are collections of photos, images, quotes, videos and anything else that positively enhances what you are attempting to achieve. It can be a collage made of cardboard and magazine clippings or a digital board you build on Pinterest or another site.

IN EITHER CASE, the purpose of the vision board is to offer positive visual support for your objective. By often looking at your vision board, you mentally train your mind to think positively about your journey. This can ease the process of making positive decisions and avoiding negativeness.

THE POWER of Hypnosis

While hypnosis may have a bad track record amongst some people thanks to carnival scams and party performers, hypnotherapy is an actual physiological procedure that is commonly used in psychology and psychiatry to treat a variety of mental conditions.

WHEN PERFORMED BY AN EXPERIENCED PROFESSIONAL, hypnosis puts the subject in a deeply relaxed trance-like state then places post- hypnotic tips into the individual's subconscious. These recommendations then become embedded into their belief system, however only if they are currently open to the tip in the first place.

YOU COULD NOT hypnotise somebody to believe in God if they are already an agnostic or atheist, or to vote Democratic if they are a Republican, for example.

. . .

SO SOMEBODY who is struggling to give up cigarette smoking can be hypnotised to think that whenever they smoke a cigarette it tastes like toxin. When the person comes out of the hypnotic state, that suggestion remains part or their belief system so whenever they smoke, the bad taste is so anxiety-causing that they are unable to complete the cigarette.

IF YOU ARE interested in utilising hypnosis to help you break your bad habit, ask your medical professional or health care expert to refer you to a respectable professional therapist.

NINE

Act

The Chinese philosopher Confucius famously said, "The journey of a thousand miles starts with a single step." Although he said those words more than 2,500 years back, they are still as real today as the day they were spoken.

NOW THAT YOU understand the 6 phases of self-change and you have a Strategy, the next step is to implement it. Making big changes in your life can be intimidating and can cause a lot of apprehension in many people, however by this point you must be positive in the concept that you really wish to make a real change in your life.

FOCUS AND DETERMINATION

THE TIME and energy you invested developing your Strategy will now settle as you begin your journey. You understand ahead of time where you require to be every action of the way and this will assist to keep you focused and motivated. Still, there are always going to be unforeseeable possibilities and life is occasionally going to throw a curveball at you.

THE RADICAL CHANGES you are making now will have favourable effects on every element of your life from here on. If you start to waver, use the strategies detailed in the last chapter-- such as affirmations, a vision board, meditation and the rest-- to continue on track.

APPLICATION

You may feel afraid or nervous when you wake up on Day 1 of your program to break your bad routine and replace it with a good one. Rest assure, as you have actually planned every action of the method. You already have all the tools you require to conquer your bad habit, plus you have retrained your mind to be positive and to decline negativeness.

ALTHOUGH THE ROAD IS LONG, you can do this! By now you are totally ready for this. You are strong, brave and capable. Newton's First Law of Physics states that things in movement tends to stay in the movement which things at rest tend to stay at rest. This law can easily be applied to habits. It's far much easier to stay the way you are instead of change. But without change, there can be no growth. And without growth, you are not going to achieve the success that you want.

THE DANGERS OF "ALL OR NOTHING"

Something is much better than absolutely nothing. Even the smallest of accomplishments is beneficial to ongoing failure. While your supreme goal might be something quite tough, it typically isn't realistic to expect you to leap from Point A to the finish line in one single step. It just doesn't work that way.

. . .

PREVENT TAKING AN "ALL OR NOTHING" approach to breaking your bad routine. It will cause absolutely nothing but aggravation. Most of the times, a bad routine can be conquered using smaller, more possible actions that are supported by positivity and continuous motivation, both external and internal.

ACCEPT INCREMENTAL IMPROVEMENTS. It's okay if you don't consume the whole enchilada in one bite. Undoubtedly, it's preferable to take small bites instead of choking to death or overburdening your digestive system. In the exact same method, it's fine to take it slowly when breaking a bad habit. Your bad routine didn't develop overnight and you shouldn't anticipate to overcome it instantly.

ACCEPTING FAILURE. For someone with a negative viewpoint, failure is something terrible, scary and should be prevented at all costs. But for the positive- believing person, failure is a chance. As people, we find out through failure. It's the "error" part of trial and error that leads to the greatest discoveries. When you have an obstacle on your journey or you fail to attain your Tactical plan's weekly goal, use it as a knowing tool to determine what went wrong and why so that you can prevent making the same mistake once again.

POWER OF PERSISTENCE

YOU CAN BE the hero of your own motion picture as long as you keep getting up and coming back for more. The magnificence isn't in the destination, it remains in the journey. By using the power of your own perseverance, you will conquer your bad habit and change it into a good one, no matter the blows you receive along the way.

65

YOU MAY NOT WIN every fight and in some cases, you are even going to get your ass kicked. However, as long as you keep fighting, you will be the champ.

TEN

Keeping Score

I n order to assure that you get the result you want and stay motivated and on track, it's important that you record your development and evaluation and refine your Strategy as you progress through your program.

YOU DREW up your Strategy from a safe range prior to you entered the heat of the action. There most likely were things that you didn't expect to occur. It's all right to make changes. Your Strategy is a guideline, not a guideline book. As long as it gets you to where you want to go within the timeframe that you have actually planned for yourself, it can be adapted and customised as much or as little as you like. Simply make certain that your program is advancing towards your goal, not backsliding back into the bad habit you are attempting to break.

A RECORD of Your Success

. . .

KEEP a record of your performance versus your Game Plan. I like to call this the "Triumph Log". This will help you measure and see your progress as you move through your program.

IN YOUR VICTORY LOG, record your efficiency versus your goal. Recognise imperfections. Be unflinching and sincere. The Success Log is for your eyes only.

ULTIMATELY, when you reach your goal, your Practice Diary and your Victory Log can assist indicate the crucial elements that led to your success. These crucial elements can then be used to other locations of your life so that you can make continuous, positive enhancements and move closer to understanding your Vision Declaration.

WEEKLY PROGRESS REVIEWS

SET up a time to examine your success each week. Make it a new practice by making it at the very same time and day every week, making it much easier to remember to do it. Eventually, you will begin to eagerly anticipate this time due to the fact that the closer you get to your objective, the more likely it will be that the news will be good.

WEEKLY PROGRESS REVIEWS need to be as non-judgmental as possible. Update your Victory Log without emotion, discussing exactly what you did well and what you didn't. Any obstacle of failure should be accompanied by a strategy to correct those areas where you require enhancement.

TAKING It to the Next Level

.   .   .

YOU'VE MADE it through your very first Strategy. You have actually broken a bad habit and changed it with a new one. Now what? You still have your Vision Declaration attain. Construct on the experience and success of your very first Strategy and use those lessons to the next bad routine you want to remedy. Where does it stop? You understand you have reached your ultimate goal when your Vision Declaration is no longer a target you want to attain, but actually describes your daily life.

BREAKING the Habit Completely

PETER IS STILL STUCK on the streets. I hope he'll be prepared to get in the pickup truck soon. In the meantime, he is still waiting on an imaginary flight to a location and time that just exist in his imagination. He still can't make a choice based upon what he needs to do today.

IF YOU HAVE ACTUALLY PERTAINED to the awareness that you're stuck in a self- defeating way of life, you have actually currently taken the primary step in the cycle of self-change. You have actually started to become conscious of the need to alter in some area of your life.

THIS MIGHT BE completion of this study, however it's not completion of the roadway for you. There are still numerous bad habits to fix prior to you are living the life you have always imagined on your own. But now that you are equipped with the knowledge of how to accomplish this, the experience of breaking your very first bad habit will give you the confidence you need to continue your journey.

.   .   .

YOU HAVE the power to do whatever you set your mind to do. Now you understand the reality of this statement. Never, ever, ever give up. You can alter your world. You just need to do it one routine at a time! Use this study as a step-by-step guide. Do not attempt to avoid any of the phases-- it will not work.

IT'S ONLY a matter of time prior to you win the war against bad habits when you win the fight in your mind.